D1235081

# TABLE OF CONTENTS

# Chapter 6: Chapter 6: Training 36

## CHAPTER 1:

# Real Scenarios

Turn on the TV on any given night, and you are bombarded with more scary, shocking and depressing news than your mind can handle. Browse the news sites and read your local paper - you'll find that frightening stories happen with an alarming regularity. You do not want to become the victim in those stories... but it could happen. You do not want to be a bystander who can do nothing to stop these terrible things from happening either, but it could happen.

**Consider the following scenario.**

It's just a little past dusk. Your children are in the family room

watching television and you are expecting your husband to arrive any time now. He met up with some friends after work, but he should be home very soon. You are in the kitchen finishing up some dishes, when you notice the floodlight has come on. As you finish washing up, you

think to yourself, that If it was your husband, he would have already been in the door by now to greet you and the kids.

The light has been on for a good five minutes, and no one has entered. Your dog is barking, and you try to calm him down. You are worried, and you open the back door to investigate. Fear grips you, and the only thing you can do is shout to see if it is your husband. Then, you hear a loud clang as something drops in the garage. You feel your heart skip a beat.

You've rehearsed the drill with your children before, and you know what to do. You lock the door and send the kids to the basement. Your son calls for the dog, who is somewhere in the house, but the dog does not respond. You do not wait. You lock the children in the basement, knowing that time is vital in these scenarios. Then, you head up to get your cellphone and gun.

You call 911 and return to the kitchen. You can see and hear the back door being jiggled. Someone is trying to get inside.

You scream, "I've got a GUN!" You know these words would paralyze anyone in their tracks. Then, you say, "I'm also on the phone with the police. You need to back away from my property NOW!"

Situations like these are all too real and I wouldn't want that to happen to anyone, especially you.

No matter where you live, alone or with a family, you need to know the gun laws and you need to know how to defend yourself and those around you.

This book will help you prepare.

Let's look at several real-life stories from the news to help illustrate just how important this can be.

 # What To Do

In a perfect world, there would be no danger and you would not need a gun to defend yourself and your home. However, we know that the real world is a violent, dangerous place. You need to be ready.

• A woman in Toledo, Ohio had been having a bad string of luck. For two mornings in a row, she had woken up to find that her car had been broken into. On the third morning, just before 5am, the woman's boyfriend left for work. He was at a gas station nearby when he saw a stranger (who seemed suspicious) walking toward his home. He called his girlfriend to warn her, and she was at the front door when this stranger tried to kick his way inside. She was armed and able to hold him at gunpoint on the ground until the police arrived. She later stated, "I'm not moving. This is my home. I will continue to protect my home. That's what the Second Amendment is for."

• In North Carolina, three men forced their way into a

3

home with the intent of robbing the family and tried to rape the young girl who was at home. Fortunately, her grandfather was home at the time. One of the men knocked on the door and said he had car trouble. While the grandfather was going to help him, two other men rushed inside and pulled out guns. They were robbing the family and going to rape the granddaughter in the back of the house when the grandfather grabbed one of the guns and opened fire on the three. He was injured, but if he'd had his own gun, he might have been able to stop the situation earlier. He killed one of the invaders and the other two were soon identified.

 # What Not To Do

In this next story, you can see the reason so many people on the other side are screaming for more gun control laws. Yes, these stories are terrifying. Yes, it is so sad that the innocent lives are lost. But we need to understand that more laws are not really going to change anything. These tragedies are preventable. You just need to use common sense and the safety rules we outline in this book.

- A three-year-old child accidently shot and killed his mother after he had found a handgun hidden under the couch in her Oklahoma home. It is tragic for everyone involved, but she also happened to be an Army veteran who should have known better. You can't keep weapons in the house in such a reckless manner. It was a recipe for disaster.

**Negligence and pure criminal intent are the main problems with guns, not whether they can hold ten rounds or twelve, and someone with criminal intent can obtain a gun, regardless of the laws.**

# CHAPTER 2:

# Guns and the Second Amendment

People in the government worry about money, getting elected, and staying in power. They do not worry about someone breaking into your home and doing you harm. That might be a hard pill to swallow, but they don't. At least not until they need something from you, like a vote in an upcoming election.

Do you really think Donald Trump cares enough about your guns and rights to make sure they are safe? He's part of the system. The government, regardless of who is in charge, is still the government. They are a large organization built to control and to give you the mere illusion of freedom. Even if Trump cared about you, he is just one man and is relatively powerless when it comes to gun laws. There are too many bad cooks in the kitchen and only your own knowledge will protect your guns.

You have a right to own and use firearms, but this is a right you will have to keep fighting to defend.

You also have the responsibility to know the laws behind firearms, how to use guns properly and safely and how to be a good ambassador and responsible gun owner. We will be covering the most essential elements you need to know as a gun owner right here in this book.

In this chapter, we will be covering some of the reasons people want to own firearms, as well as what the Second Amendment is and what it means. You can use this information not only to increase your own knowledge, but to help others to learn as well.

# Should I Own A Gun?

Should you own a gun? People may ask you why you own firearms or why they should own firearms. Some are genuinely curious. Others have a prejudice or blind hate when it comes to firearms.

These questions are usually asked by someone who is not a gun owner and someone who may have never fired a weapon before. They often have no knowledge of weapons. They think the "AR" in AR15 stands for "Assault Rifle" and have no concept of what semi-automatic means. There are people out there who don't know the difference between a rifle and a machine gun. And of course there are those who nearly faint at a mere mention of a firearm.

As gunowners, we should be ambassadors for firearms. Weapons themselves are not dangerous. Those with bad intentions are the problem...

So, back to the main question. Why should you own a gun?

# 1. Safety

For starters, you have the right to defend yourself, your family, and your property. A firearm helps you do this by leveling the playing field. Many criminals out there have firearms and would not hesitate to use them on you and your loved ones.

The world is a dangerous place and anyone who tells you differently lives in an ivory tower... which probably has armed guards patrolling the entrance.

Having a firearm – and knowing how to use it properly in dangerous situations – can make a world of difference. However, owning a firearm goes beyond just safety and defense.

# 2. Hunting

Some people like to go hunting. They hunt for meat, which they can use to feed themselves and their families. Hunting is a long-standing tradition in the United States, and firearms, rightfully, are a big part of that.

# 3. Target Shooting

Others enjoy target shooting and the challenge it presents. Some just shoot for fun, while others are professional level competitors competing for glory, fame, prizes, and sponsorships.

# 4. Collection

Still, others like the idea of collecting interesting and unique firearms. Some people like coins or stamps... others like guns.

There's nothing wrong with that and they should be punished for their interest.

## 4. You Have The *Right* To Bear Arms

As a citizen of the United States, you have the right to bear arms. In fact, you don't have

to give a reason for wanting to own a gun even if someone asks.

# What Is the Second Amendment and What Does It Say?

The Founding Fathers of this nation put in a lot of thought and effort into the creation of the United States Constitution. They wanted to ensure our fledgling nation would not make the same mistakes as other nations in the past. Namely, they wanted the government to be by the people and for the people. Last thing they wanted was monarchs or tyrants running the show.

To assist with this, they created the Bill of Rights - the first ten amendments to the Constitution, that were adopted and ratified all at the same time. The First Amendment included the right to free speech, freedom of religion regardless of what your religion might be, freedom of the press, and the right to peaceably assemble.

The amendment that will concern us the most in this book is the Second Amendment or *the right to keep and bear arms.* The amendment states,

*"A well-regulated Militia, being necessary to the security of a free state, the right of the people to keep and bear arms, shall not be infringed."*

Some have tried to say that this was only meant for military usage, but that's simply not the case. Historic usage of the term, even before the Bill of Rights, means to keep and bear private arms.

In the Seton Hall Constitutional Law Journal in 1995, Sayoko Blodgett-Ford wrote "The Changing Meaning of the Right to Bear Arms".

In this piece, he cites a pamphlet that was circulating around the time of the Pennsylvania ratifying convention. In the pamphlet, written at the time of the Bill of Rights, a passage reads "The people have a right to bear arms for the defense of themselves and their own state, or the United States, or the purpose of killing game; and no law shall be passed for disarming the people or any of them, unless for crimes committed."
Now, when you read that passage from the pamphlet, it is clear. People should absolutely have the right to bear arms unless they have committed a crime. Only then should they have that right taken away.

Taking away rights before someone commits a crime or taking away rights from an entire group of people who have done no wrong is ludicrous. Yet, that's what some out there want to have happen. Some are under the delusion that making firearms illegal will somehow curb violent crime and make the world a better place. People were hurting one another long before we discovered gunpowder. Not having a gun will not stop those who are intent on doing harm.

We've seen this time and again when people have used bombs, vehicles, knives, poison, and more, to commit terrible acts. A man recently killed two men on a train in Portland with a knife. Bad guys do bad things. Criminals don't play by the rules. They will always have access to guns because they do not obtain them through legal channels. Prohibition of alcohol did not work and neither will prohibition of firearms. The only thing it would do is make the world a more dangerous place than it already is.

The Second Amendment is in place for a reason. We can't let politicians strip us of the rights that we need for our defense, hunting and sport.

# Let's Learn More About the Laws and Your Responsibility as a Gun Owner

Over the course of this book, we will be looking at many aspects of gun ownership, including how to be responsible as a gun owner, the current federal and state laws, safety, training, and more. We want you to know how to handle a gun and we want you to know your rights.

## CHAPTER 3:

# Gun Law Basics and Recent Changes to the Gun Laws

It's mind boggling that some people believe having even more gun laws, or stricter gun laws, will somehow curb gun violence. The guns themselves are not violent. Rather, it is the people who wield them that dictate what happens with a gun.

More laws will do nothing but hamper the ability of law abiding citizens to obtain the guns they want for hunting, target practice and defense.

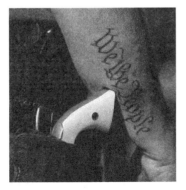

Criminals are criminals because they do not abide by the law. Those who have the intention of harming someone will do so whether they have a gun or not. After all, murder is illegal and there are still plenty of murders committed daily.

Criminals don't care about laws,

so why keep making more of them? Instead, it makes more sense to use the laws that are already in place to keep criminals out of the public rather than guns out of the hands of honest citizens. Unfortunately, that's not the way some people think, and there are proposals in the works to pass more restrictive laws against guns.

Interestingly though, as we look at the statistics for the states that have strict gun laws, we find that gun crimes there are rampant.

We are already subject to many gun laws. It is important that you take the time to understand those laws. Know how they pertain to you on a federal level, as well as a state level. In this chapter, we will be looking at each of these, including some of the most recent gun laws to make it onto the books. In addition, we will look at helping you to understand a major loophole in the law. These insights can put you at a big advantage over your neighbors when it comes to understanding what you can and can't do.

# The Legal Definition
# of a Firearm

Do you really know what a firearm is? By understanding the legal definition, you will find there is a lot of flexibility and freedom in the law.

According to 18 USC §921(3), a firearm is "Any weapon

(including a starter gun) which will expel a projectile by means of an explosive or is designed or may be readily converted to do so. This includes the frame or receiver of any such weapon, any firearm muffler or silencer or any destructive device. A "destructive device" includes any explosive, incendiary or poison gas --- (i)bomb; (ii) grenade or (iii) similar device, or any combination of parts designed or intended to be converted into a destructive device, or from which a destructive device may be readily assembled. Does not include black powder or antique type firearms."

# Who Is Eligible to Own a Gun in the United States?

While it is a right to own a firearm, that does not truly mean that everyone can have a gun. Those who are eligible to possess and own firearms include United States citizens and permanent resident aliens. Other exceptions apply certain non-immigrant aliens admitted to the United States who want to lawfully hunt or those who have one of the following exceptions.

• Valid hunting license or permit in a US state.

- Official representative of a foreign government "accredited to the United States Government or the Government's mission to an international organization having its headquarters in the United States or is en route to or from another country to which that alien is accredited."

- Official of a foreign government, or distinguished foreign visitor designated by the Department of State.

- Foreign law enforcement officer of friendly foreign government who enters the U.S. on law enforcement business.

- Has received a waiver from the Attorney General, "if the waiver petition shows it would be in the interests of justice and would not jeopardize the public safety under 18 U.S. Code § 922(y)(3)(c)."

# Federal Gun Laws

It is impossible to cover all the federal gun laws in a single book of, but what we will do here is offer a quick reference for the key provisions.

### *Possession of a Firearm or Ammunition by a Prohibited Person 18 USC § 922(g) & (n)*

This is punishable by a prison sentence of up to 10 years and it could be a minimum of 15 if the offender has three or more prior convictions for a felony crime of violence. This would include things such as assault, burglary, murder, etc. and/or a drug trafficking felony.

They would be charged if they have (A) possession of or take receipt of firearms or ammo, and if they are (B) considered a prohibited person. These include:

- Felon
- Drug user/addict
- Alien
- Is subject to a domestic restraining order
- Has prior convictions for domestic assault
- Is a fugitive from justice
- Has a dishonorable discharge from the military; AND

(C) The firearm or ammo has been transported across state lines at any time.

**Knowingly Sell, Give or Otherwise Dispose of Any Firearm or Ammunition to Any Person Who Falls Within One of the Above Categories, 18 USC § 922(d)**

This would be punishable by up to 10 years in prison.

**Use, Carry, or Possess a Firearm in Relation to or in Furtherance of a Drug Felony or a Federal Crime of Violence 18 USC § 924(c)**

The minimum punishment of this crime is five years and it can be as high as life in prison without parole. It could also result in the death penalty if a death occurs as the result of using a firearm.

It is important to keep in mind that the mandatory minimum can increase based on the type of firearm that is used. For example, using a silencer/suppressor, sawed off shotgun and similar weapons can increase the minimum sentence length.

In addition, the minimum time can increase based on whether there were additional offenses committed and whether the gun was discharged, brandished or just possessed.

### *Stolen Firearm, Ammunition, or Explosive, 18 USC §§842(h); 922(i), (j) & (u)*

This is punishable by up to 10 years in prison. A person may not "receive, possess, conceal, store, pledge or accept as security for a loan, barter, sell or ship or transport across a state line any stolen firearm, ammunition or explosive."

In addition, a person "May not steal or unlawfully take or carry away a firearm from the person or premises of a firearms licensee."

### *Firearm in a School Zone, 18 USC § 922(q)(2)(A)*
Discharging or possessing a firearm in a school zone, except as authorized, is punishable by up to five years in prison.

### *Knowingly Possess or Manufacture, 18 USC § 922(k), (o) & (v); 26 USC § 5861*

Violating this law is punishable by up to five to ten years in prison based on the violation. You are not allowed to manufacture or possess any of the following items.

- Machine gun, fully automatic firearm or any part designed or intended exclusively for use in such a weapon

- Any firearm silencer, including any device, or part thereof, designed to silence, muffle, or diminish the

report of a firearm
• Sawed-off shotgun with a barrel length of less than 18" or overall length of less than 26"

• Sawed-off rifled with a barrel length of less than 16" or overall length less than 26"

• Destructive device

• Semi-automatic assault weapon manufactured after October 1, 1991

• Any firearm which lacks a serial number or contains an altered or obliterated serial number

### Sell, Deliver, or Transfer to a Juvenile, 18 USC § 922(x)(1) and 18 USC § 922(b)

Violation of this law is punishable by up to a year in prison, unless the person who transfers the weapon had a reason to believe the underage person would commit a violent crime with gun or ammunition provided to them. Then, it would be up to ten years in prison. If a firearms licensee does this, they would face up to five years in prison.

No one can sell, deliver, or transfer handguns or handgun-only ammunition to anyone who is under 18 years old. Those who are under 18 may not possess a handgun or handgun-only ammunition. However, there are some exceptions to the preceding two provisions of the law – including when a juvenile has written permission from the parent.

A firearms licensee may not sell any gun or ammunition to anyone under the age of 18 and may not sell a handgun or handgun ammunition to a person under the age of 21.

## More Laws to Know

• The Brady Handgun Violence Prevention Act of1993 requires background checks for most firearm purchases depending on the venue and the seller.

• The Federal Assault Weapons Ban was active from 1994 to 2004 and banned semiautomatic assault weapons along with "large capacity ammunition feeding devices". This law expired in 2004.

• The Protection of Lawful Commerce in Arms Act in 2005 ensured that manufacturers of firearms, as well as licensed dealers, were not held liable for negligence when crimes were committed using their products.

Many of the federal laws can be prosecuted under state law. However, the punishments under the federal law tend to be more severe. For this reason, many illegal firearms arrests end up getting turned over to the feds from the local and state authorities.

## State Gun Laws

State gun laws are meant to help regulate the sales, possession and use of firearms and ammunition. The laws of the states, territories and the District of Columbia varyquite a bit. It is impossible to cover all the laws in this book, so it is vital that you research your state firearm laws regarding. In some instances, the laws of the state are less restrictive than federal laws. However, in other cases, they are more restrictive, sometimes bordering on ridiculous.

One of the most troubling issues about state laws is that only 44 of our states have provisions in their state constitutions that echo the Second Amendment. The states without this provision include California, Iowa, Maryland, Minnesota, New Jersey, and New York. These states do not seem to hold the Second Amendment in very high regard. However, NY does have civil rights laws that have a provision akin to the Second Amendment.

It's fortunate that we have the Second Amendment at the federal level. However, some of the laws that have been enacted, particularly in California, show the state's disdain for guns and law-abiding gun owners. Again, we'll cover some of these in the next section.

As a gun owner, you are responsible for understanding gun laws in your state. Those in California need to be especially careful.

## Recent Changes to Gun Laws

California has a wide range of gun laws that frequently seem

to punish legitimate gun owners rather than criminals.

One of the most recent California laws to have passed, thanks to Governor Jerry Brown, is the requirement for a background check for anyone who is purchasing ammunition. In addition, there will be a $50 permit fee for the purchase of ammunition. This makes buying ammunition a massive hassle for those who are using their guns legally. In addition, the new law will allow tracking of anyone who buys more than 3,000 rounds at a gun shop.

The state has outlawed rifles that have a detachable magazine. All rifles owned by those in California will now be required to have attached magazines loaded one round at a time. This makes little sense, as it has been proven that you can still load a five- round attached magazine extremely quickly.

California has also banned the purchase of semiautomatic rifles that have what legislators call "evil features". This refers to bullet buttons that make it simpler to change magazines (which won't be allowed at all soon), flash hiders and pistol grips.

Of course, there are plenty of guns in the hands of criminals already. They are not going to abide by the law – they obtain guns illegally anyway. At the end of the day, the laws seem to hamper the law-abiding gun owner while they do nothing to stop criminals.

Strangely, the government of California still equates the weapons on sale today with assault weapons, which were banned in 1989. No true assault weapons are available for sale to the public. However, this legislation is looking for features that could identify a semiautomatic rifle specifically as an assault rifle. Essentially, California is trying to profile rifles. If a gun looks like an actual assault rifle used in the military, they want to ban it.

If a criminal wants to kill someone and needs ammunition,

do you think the new ammunition law would stop them? Do you think a criminal will turn over his AK-47 or MAC-10 because it is against the law? Do you think adding to these laws is going to make anyone safe? Criminals break the law... it's just what they do.

If you live in California, visit the California Stand and Fight page for most current updates on the California's gun laws: *https://www.nraila.org/campaigns/2017/california/stand-and-fight-california/*

## Positive Changes

Of course, not all laws are bad. Let's look at some of the recent changes to the laws in Tennessee. In the past, you needed to be 21 to obtain a carry permit for handguns in the state. However, a recently passed law would allow those who are under 21 and who are active military, retired, or honorably discharged to get a carry permit. They only need to prove that they are eligible.

Tennessee enacted this law because they were motivated by the 2015 terror attack in Chattanooga where Muhammad Yousef Abdulazeez murdered five members of the military who were at a recruiting station.

In addition, Tennessee changed the cost of a lifetime handgun permit from $500 to $200 for those who are renewing. For those who are applying for the first time, the cost will be $315.

In Ohio, there were some changes to the laws as well thanks to Senate Bill 199. Those who have concealed carry licenses are now allowed to carry their firearm to more locations, including non-secure areas of airports, private planes and daycare facilities. In addition, employees are now allowed to store their guns and ammo in their vehicles while they are at work.

Concealed carry on college campuses is still not allowed, but the colleges are able to authorize certain people or groups to carry weapons on campus if they choose. Daycare centers also have the right to post a no gun sign if they do not want anyone bringing firearms onto their property.

## *Learn the Firearm Transportation Laws*

In addition to the basic laws of ownership and carry, you should also check to determine the laws for transporting firearms in motor vehicles. Even if you do not carry, open or concealed, you will still need to transport firearms if you ever plan to go hunting or to the range.

Each state and town has its own regulations so whether you are transporting guns across town or across state lines, know your responsibilities and keep yourself out of trouble.

The NRA has a great resource – "Guide to the Interstate Transportation of Firearms." It is available here: https://www.nraila.org/articles/20150101/guide-to-the-interstate-transportation and we highly recommend that you take the time to read it.

## *Stay up to date on gun laws*

Know the current federal laws. Know the laws in your state and jurisdiction and keep an eye on the laws that are being proposed. These could affect you and other gun owners. Often, politicians will try to sneak new gun laws in or pass laws through fully considering all the consequences. We are currently seeing this in California.

To find what laws are currently in the works on a federal level, visit http://www.congress.gov and filter laws by "subject – Policy Area." You can also use search words like "violence", "firearms", "ammunition". You can also visit www.usa.gov for current laws of the land.

Another great resource is the NRA Institute for Legislative Action - https://www.nraila.org/. Here you can find the latest news regarding guns and gun laws, opinion, articles and more recommended reading.

To keep up with state gun laws, visit your state government website and review your state constitution, search for "state legislature" and "proposed legislature", look at the "meeting notes" and search for "executive orders" by your state Governor.

In today's world, you need to be vigilant to make sure your rights are not being infringed upon by the government that. You may even find that you want to become active in campaigning for or against certain laws.

## The Legal Loophole

Federal law currently has a loophole that allows people to buy firearms through private sellers. This has been called the gun show loophole, private sale loophole, and private sale exemption. It is possible for any person to "sell a firearm to an unlicensed resident of the state where they reside, as long as they do not know or have reasonable cause to believe the person is prohibited from receiving or possessing firearms."

Private party sellers do not have to perform background checks on buyers at a gun show or any other venue. In addition, they are not required to record the sale or ask for identification.

In the past, this loophole worked no matter where you lived. However, there are many states that now require background checks that go beyond the federal law and that will supersede it.

Currently, a background check by a FFL (Federal Firearms License) holder is required for a private sale for all firearms in California, Colorado, Connecticut, Delaware, the District of Columbia, New York, Nevada, Oregon, Rhode Island, and Washington. You need to have a state-issued permit for all firearms in Hawaii, Illinois, Massachusetts, and New Jersey.

A background check by a FFL holder is needed for sales of handguns in Maryland and Pennsylvania. Those who live in Iowa, Michigan, Nebraska and North Carolina need to have a state-issued permit for their handguns.

Here's the Federal form for the FFL background check for your reference: *https://www.atf.gov/file/61446/download*

In the states mentioned, the loophole is not going to work for you. However, going through private sales and gun shows can still be a fantastic way to save money on the firearms you want to purchase.

At www.gunshows-usa.com, you can find up-to-date listings of upcoming gun shows across the country. You can filter them by states or months.

## CHAPTER 4:

# Gun Ownership – Overview of the Key Considerations

I n this short chapter, I just wanted to give you a brief overview of some of the key factors you need to consider as a gun owner - namely abilities, personal situation, training, safety and gun selection.

We will then be covering each of these different elements in greater detail in chapters 5, 6, 7, 8 and 9.

### Abilities
Your abilities include your mental and physical capacity to use a firearm and everything this could entail. For example, a potential mental illness could preclude some people from owning firearms. Likewise, not everyone has the mental capacity needed to fire a gun in self-defense or the physical capacity to handle a firearm.

### Personal Situation
In this chapter, we discuss issues such as your family and your location. Do you have small children? How will you keep the guns safe and out of the hands of kids and thieves, but still

easy enough for you to access? What are the laws in your location regarding owning weapons and carrying weapons? Is someone in your family against guns?

## Training

In this chapter, we will cover topics such as general knowledge of firearms, the required training you need to complete before you buy and handle firearms and other types of training that is beneficial, but not necessarily required to own a gun.

## Safety

Safety is one of the prime concerns of anyone who owns a firearm and we will be dedicating this chapter to ensuring you know how to keep yourself and your loved ones safe. You will also learn about gun storage options.

## Gun Selection

Do you know which guns are best for different situations? Do you know what firearms you can afford? Plenty of factors can come into play when it comes to choosing your firearms and we will discuss these in the chapter on selecting guns for hunting, defense and more.

## CHAPTER 5:

# Abilities and Personal Situation

**H**ow able are you when it comes to using a firearm? Ability, both mental and physical, is a factor in gun ownership. It is important to have a good understanding of your own abilities when you are considering buying a firearm.

## Mental Abilities

We can break down mental abilities into two subcategories – your mental capacity to handle a firearm responsibly and your

mental ability to handle a firearm in a defensive situation. These are very different and we will be looking at both.

### Owning/Possessing a Firearm

There are laws in place at the federal and state level when it comes to possession of a firearm by a person who is considered mentally ill. We've included this law in this section rather than the earlier section on laws because of its pertinence to this area.

Under 18 U.S.C. § 922(d), it is illegal to sell or otherwise dispose of any firearm or ammunition to another party knowing or having reasonable cause to believe he or she "has been adjudicated as a mental defective or has been committed to any mental institution."

Please keep in mind the laws in your own state regarding firearm ownership for those who are mentally ill. Let's look at a couple of state law examples.

- Illinois – A person cannot possess a firearm or ammunition if they have been a patient in a mental hospital within the last five years or is considered mentally retarded.

- Indiana – In the state of Indiana, it is illegal for someone to possess firearms or ammunition if he or she is mentally incompetent.

- Connecticut – A person cannot receive a handgun eligibility certificate if he or she was discharged from custody within the last 20 years after being found guilty of a crime that was due to mental disease or if they have been confined to a mental hospital with people who have psychiatric disabilities within the last 12 months by a probate court's order.

- Ohio – It is illegal to have, carry, acquire, or use a

firearm in this state if they have been under adjudication for mental incompetence, are mentally defective, have been committed to a mental institution, have been found to be mentally ill subject to hospitalization by court order or is an involuntary mentally ill patient.

You can see that the states may have some similarities in their laws regarding mental health when owning and using a firearm. California, again, has some of the most stringent regulations.

However, in cases of serious mental illness, we all agree it is safer to prohibit ownership and access to firearms. If someone is not competent enough to learn how to use firearms properly, they should not have access to them.

## Using a Firearm for Defense

You also need to consider whether you have the mental ability needed to use the weapon as a means of defense. Many people might think that they do, but being in a real-world scenario is much different from what you may think.

Sure, everyone imagines that he or she is the hero when something bad happens. They see themselves taking out the bad without breaking a sweat. Please understand, it doesn't usually happen that way in real life.

In real life, being frightened is very natural. Unless you have been in a firefight or shot at, you have no idea what it is truly like and you can't guarantee how you will react. You do not know the fear and uncertainty that you need to overcome if you expect to act and do the right thing without causing harm to anyone who is innocent.

You need to be honest about your abilities when it comes to actually using a firearm in defense of yourself and others.

Ideally, you will get training that can help improve your skills and increase your confidence in tense situations. We will discuss this in another chapter.

The good news is that most people have a self-preservation instinct that will allow them to overcome their fears and do the right thing to help themselves and others. For some people, this is innate. For others, it isn't. Proper training will help to ensure that you develop this ability. Gun owners just need to make sure they are not in the "Rambo mindset". The world isn't an action film and a bullet to the shoulder in real life is more than a "flesh wound."

Hopefully, you will never be in a firefight. We would love for you to live out a long and peaceful life without having to fire your weapon in self-defense. If you do need to use your weapon and you do injure or kill someone who is trying to harm you, it can take a toll on your psyche.

Those who have been in these real-life situations and who have had to take another life, whether they are a soldier, a police officer, a concealed carry gun owner or anyone else, may find that it takes a long time to come to terms with what happened. Many suffer from PTSD. That's not a sign of weakness. It's a sign of your humanity. If you have been in a situation where this has happened, seek out help and someone you can talk to..

## *Physical Abilities*

Mental abilities are just part of what you need to consider as a gun owner. You also need to think about your physical abilities, as well as any physical disabilities. Ideally, you will have the physical stamina, as well as the manual dexterity needed to load, unload and fire your gun, as well as clean your gun.

## Disabilities

You do not need to have all your limbs to be a gun owner. You do not need to be able to walk either. Physical limitations and handicaps might make things more difficult for some, but they should not preclude you from owning firearms. Never count someone out just because they have a handicap, either.

## Physical Shape

Being in great shape is not a prerequisite for gun ownership, but being fit and healthy is essential for both survival applications and everyday life.

If you are a hunter or out in the field shooting targets, it's more enjoyable if you are fit – you last longer, you are more competitive, and you feel better when you are done. If you just

want a better chance at survival in a dangerous situation, being in shape is essential. Even shooting some of the guns requires physical fitness and coordination, so don't discount your fitness. Find activities you enjoy when it comes to getting exercise and make it a part of your life. When you are healthier, you will feel better, have more energy for shooting and hunting and you will feel more confident.

## Your Personal Situation

We get it. You love your family and you want them to be safe. You also may want to supplement the food your family eats with game that you hunt. But before you bring a gun in your house, you need to think about your current personal situation. This includes where you live and what your family life is like. Let's take a closer look...

## Gun Shy Family members

If you have family members who are against guns being in the house, you could run into a bit of a problem. If it is a spouse who feels this way, you probably would have been better served speaking with him or her about this long before you got married.

Regardless of which family member is against guns, one of the best things you can do is educate him or her. People often have misconceptions about firearms that they have grown up with or have been instilled by the media. You can help to set the story straight, show them how safe guns can be and even take them to a range to shoot.

## Safety

Safety is of the utmost importance when you have firearms in the house. Your firearms need to be in a location where children, including teens, cannot freely access them. You will need to have gun lockers or safes to help with this. You also want to make sure your family knows gun safety rules and respects firearms.

"A gun is not a toy" might be cliché, but it is very true. It is something that needs to be instilled in everyone in the family. We will discuss safety in detail in another chapter.

## Location

Safety is of the utmost importance when you have firearms in the house. Your firearms need to be in a location where children, including teens, cannot freely access them. You will need to have gun lockers or safes to help with this. You also want to make sure your family knows gun safety rules and that they respect firearms.

"A gun is not a toy" might be cliché, but it is very true. It is something that needs to be instilled in everyone in the family. We will discuss more about safety in a later chapter.

## Location

Your location is also a huge factor when it comes to gun ownership, as well as what you can and can't do with a firearm. Some states have far more strict gun laws than others.
In some locations, you might not even be able to buy a particular type of hunting rifle. If you are in California, for example, you might not be able to buy a rifle with a removable magazine for hunting.

Study state gun laws, concealed and open carry laws for various locations in the state and local ordinances that may affect you before you buy a gun.

For example, in the past, it was common to see people driving around with a gun in a rack in the back of their truck. Is this still legal where you live? Do you need to keep your firearm elsewhere while transporting it?

Also, even if you have a concealed carry license, that does not mean you can carry your gun concealed everywhere you go. There may be places that have their own rules when it comes to carrying. Make sure you know these rules as well, so there are no problems when you are out at dinner, shopping or a movie. Know absolutely everything about your location when it comes to gun ownership. It is a good idea to print off key provisions of state and local regulations and put them in an envelope in your glove box. If you are ever confronted, you will be able to reference the law.

If you have questions, talk to a local gun shop owner. These

men and women rely on understanding gun laws to support their livelihood. Their insight is priceless.

# CHAPTER 6:

# Training

Y ou have the right to buy a gun. You also have a responsibility to learn how to use it safely. Simply put, you need to have training. There is more to firing a gun than just pulling the trigger. In fact, there is more to pulling the trigger than many people realize.

In this chapter, we will be covering the types of training and knowledge you need and will provide you with basic tips on how to develop your skills.

## *General Knowledge*

You need to start with the basics, like understanding gun terminology, how a gun works, and how to fire it safely. A good beginner course would be one where you do not do any actual shooting. Instead, you get instruction on the basic skills – like safe handling and storage of firearms and ammunition – and on the proper gun etiquette and attitude.

## Parts of the Firearm

While each gun is different, most firearms are made up of the same basic parts – muzzle, breech, hammer and trigger.

• Muzzle – This is the opening at the front of the firearm where the projectile leaves the gun.

• Breech – The breech is the back of the gun. In the past, guns were all loaded through the muzzle. New technologies allowed for breech-loading firearms, which made the loading process faster, simpler, and more convenient.

• This is the part of the firearm that hits the primer on the ammunition. When it strikes the primer, it causes the powder to ignite. The bullet or pellets will then  be propelled out of the muzzle. The hammer can be internal or external. Keep in mind that in some cases, the hammer does not have to contact the primer – a firing pin is struck by the hammer, which then drives the pin into the primer to fire the round.

• Trigger – The trigger is the part of the firearm that the user squeezes to fire the weapon.

## Assault Rifle/Assault Weapon

An **assault rifle** is a military weapon. You will not find these in the hands of civilians, unless those civilians happen to be criminals who have somehow stolen those weapons. This is very different from the term a**ssault weapon**, although the two are often used interchangeably, which is, of course, incorrect.

The term **assault weapon** was created by politicians and is loved by the media. The definition tends to change based on jurisdiction and many times it is used to reflect the appearance of the weapon rather than the actual power or function of the weapon. Keep in mind that there are .22 caliber rifles out there that look like military style weapons, but they are still just a semi-automatic .22 caliber.

## AR-15

The AR-15 is a very popular type of semi-automatic rifle. It is reliable, fun to shoot, and relatively easy to maintain. However, this firearm has such a bad reputation today. It is essentially the pit bull of firearms. The difference is that a pit bull can act on its own accord, while a firearm can't.

In addition, many people believe that AR stands for assault rifle. However, it stands for Armalite, the name of the manufacturer that first built the rifle.

## Safe and Safety

These terms have several different meanings. A safe could be the physical safe in which you keep your firearms. It can also refer to the gun being "safe", meaning the safety is engaged.

Safety can refer to being conscious about the rules of safety when you are handling a firearm. It can also refer to the mechanical device that is used to block the firing pin or the trigger so the gun cannot be fired.

## Silencer

The term silencer is something of a misnomer and the actual term that should be used is suppressor. This is a device that can be affixed to the firearm to suppress the sound. It does not actually silence the firearm, as movies and television might have you believe. It merely changes the sound characteristics.

## Caliber

The term caliber is used to denote the size of a bullet a gun will fire. It could be denoted in millimeters, such as 9mm or 10mm, or it could be denoted as .40 caliber, for example. Often, letters or words accompany the caliber and denote the brand name or abbreviation for the company that first created the round. For example, .40 S&W.

## Cartridge

A cartridge is the combination of the bullet and the powder, along with the primer and casing. Some of the other terms often used interchangeably with cartridge include shell, ammo, and round.

## Magazine

A magazine is a type of ammunition feeding device that is found with a repeating firearm. Some magazines are detachable and can carry various amounts of ammunition. Other times, they are permanently attached to the firearm.

## Semi-automatic vs. Automatic

For those who do not know much about firearms, there tends to be a substantial amount of confusion when it comes to semi-automatic vs. automatic firearms. Often, people cannot tell the difference and that includes journalists who are writing about these firearms – often trying to show them in a negative light.

Semi-automatic means that the firearm can fire repeatedly. However, it requires the user to squeeze the trigger and release it for each shot. An automatic firearm is one that will continue firing so long as the user is holding down the trigger and there is still ammunition in the gun.

Many people who are not in the know believe that all rifles that have a military-style appearance are going to fire automatically. That is why so many of the uninformed believe that all these rifles are machine guns. They never bother to learn the difference and instead spread disinformation.

## Learn More

One of the things you will notice in this book is that we often encourage you to learn more. That's because there are so much to learn about when it comes to firearms, so make sure you educate yourself.

## Required Training

Training may not always be required by law before you are able to buy a firearm. It depends on the state you live in and the type of firearm you are buying. In some areas, though, you are required to take some basic training for firearms, which includes safety.

The instructors make sure you know how to load and unload the firearm and the basic safety rules (which we will discuss later in the book).

Because states can differ when it comes to required training, we urge you to check with your own state to determine just what you need to do to own a firearm. For example, in some states, such as Massachusetts, all first-time firearm license applicants are required to take either a MA Certified Firearm Safety Course or a Basic Hunter Education Course. Find the requirements in your state and then find a facility that can provide you with the training and the documentation you need.

NRA has a great online training website where you can get some gun training without leaving your house: https://onlinetraining. nra.org/

## *Cleaning*

Most people are excited about getting their first firearm, but they don't learn how to clean it properly. You do not have to take any classes to learn how to clean a rifle, shotgun, or handgun, as you can find plenty of videos on YouTube and on private blogs.

• The NRA-FAMILY website has a simple general gun-cleaning guide here: https://www.nrafamily.org/articles/2017/3/26/ barrel-bliss-how-*to-properly-clean-a- gun/*

• This article by Guns and Ammo will show you how to properly clean a handgun: *http://www. gunsandammo.com/home-featured/ga-basics-how-to-clean-your- handgun/*

• Here's a great shotgun cleaning

guide by Game Bird Hunts: *http://www.gamebirdhunts.com/ Resources/FeaturedArticles/HowtoProperlyClean aShotgun/ tabid/585/Default.aspx*

• Instructables.com has this great instructable on cleaning a rifle: *http://www.instructables.com/id/How-to-Clean-A-Bolt-Action-Rifle/*

Ultimately, you will want to find the proper cleaning instructions for your make an model. You will be happy you did - a clean gun will be reliable and stay in great shape for years to come.

## Beyond Required Training

If your state has required courses, you probably want to do more than simply learn the basics. Let's look at some of the diverse types of training options that are out there to see what might pique your interest. Keep in mind that many of the classes feature classroom learning, or e-learning in some cases, as well as practice in the field.

## Pistol Courses

Some popular pistol courses include the basics of pistol shooting, defensive pistol techniques and even marksman simulator training. In addition, there are concealed carry courses, which you would have to take and be able to pass

before you could be granted a concealed carry permit in many locations.

## Rifle Courses

Rifle training courses can be helpful for those who want to learn how to defend themselves and their property, as well as those who want to improve their hunting skills. Basic rifle shooting courses will help you to become better acquainted with your firearm, while more advanced training will teach you how to shoot accurately in different positions and at varying distances.

## *Shotgun Courses*

Shotguns are popular choices for home defense, as well as for hunting and skeet shooting. A basic shotgun course will provide you with the knowledge and skills needed for hitting a moving target, while remaining safe and conscious of your surroundings.

## *Tactical Training and Personal Protection*

Personal protection courses and tactical training courses provide you with the knowledge and techniques needed to make it easier for you to protect yourself and your family in various situations. You can learn how to avoid dangerous encounters, which is always the goal, as well as how to use your firearms for defense if the need arises.

Tactical training can take many forms and is a good option for those who want to improve their skills and knowledge. Bodyguards, executives and the like can often find benefits in these tactical courses.

## *Finding a Great Instructor*

You need to make sure you are working with a qualified instructor who can teach you the proper marksmanship skills you need. He or she can instill good habits when it comes to safety, target acquisition and more.

A good instructor will provide you with a solid foundation and increase your confidence over time. This will help you in self-defense situations, hunting and even when you are just practicing at the range.

Looking for a great instructor? Here's what to do.

## Ask Others

One of the best and simplest ways to find an instructor is to ask other shooters for some recommendations. Make sure you let them know you want a professional instructor and not just someone who can give you a few pointers.

## Research Your Area

You should also take the time to research your area for professional instructors and companies offering firearms training in your area. Later in the book, you will find links for training facilities in each state. It's not a comprehensive list, but it will help you get started.

## Private Lessons

Something else to consider when you are choosing an instructor is private vs. group lessons. One of the benefits is that you will have one-on-one time with the instructor (or with several instructors in some cases), which can make it easier to learn. You can often learn more, since you do not have to wait for everyone in the class to grasp certain concepts and techniques. Private lessons will cost more, but are the best way to get specialized training beyond the basics and get personalized tips.

# 7 Secrets for Better Shooting

### Secret #1: Close-Range Drills

This is a relatively simple drill and one you should practice regularly for several reasons.

First, the close-range drills with a target between four and five yards away will typically replicate the distance of self-defense engagements. Practice at this range while trying to get the bullets in as tight of a group as possible. Ideally, they will be in the same hole – that is the goal. You will improve your accuracy and gun control, which can help you when you shoot targets at further ranges.

## Secret #2: Ball and Dummy Drills

Ball ammo is live ammo, while dummy ammo, as the name suggests, isn't. Using a ball and dummy drill can help you eliminate flinch when shooting.

Many people do not realize just how much they anticipate recoil when they are firing and this can severely throw off their accuracy. By combining a magazine with dummy and ball ammo, you can get a better idea of just how much you might be flinching when you shoot. It might surprise you just how much the muzzle of the gun moves and this will throw off your shot.

This drill will also help you work on your concentration and technique. Eventually, it will eliminate the flinch and make you more accurate. This drill will work with rifles and handguns alike.

## Secret #3: Practice Proper Trigger Control

One of the big problems that affects novice shooters, and even those who have been shooting for a while, is improper trigger control. They are pulling the trigger, often with the crook of their finger. When you shoot this way, it alters the direction of the muzzle slightly, which will throw off your shots. Before you blame the firearm for not being accurate, you need to make sure you are utilizing proper trigger control.

The correct method is to squeeze the trigger, typically with the fat part of your finger. You want to concentrate and squeeze smoothly without tensing up while you are waiting for the recoil. Bring the trigger straight back to fire the shot without hesitation. It takes practice, but proper trigger control will drastically improve your skills.

## Secret #4: Rely on the Front Sight and Target
When you are lining up your target, you want to practice fast acquisition using the front sight and placing it on the target. Ready up drills can help with this. With this type of drill, you will raise the firearm, acquire the target via the front sight, fire, and lower the weapon.

Then, you will repeat this process until the gun is empty.

Requiring target acquisition with each round that you fire makes you rely more on the front sight until it becomes second nature. This drill should be practiced regularly.

## Secret #5: Moving Targets
Going to the range and shooting at still targets will provide you with the foundation you need as a shooter. However, when you are trying to shoot a moving target, it is quite different. Try to find a range that offers moving targets for the added challenge they provide.

After all, if you are in a real-world situation, you can be sure your targets are not going to be standing still. In some real-world situations, the target could be rushing right towards you or even firing back..

## *Secret #6: Record Your Sessions*

Here's another tip that can be quite useful and it is one that many people do not every think to do. Whenever you head out to the range or the field to go shooting, you should make it a point to record your sessions. Most people have video cameras right on their phone, and if you don't, you can always get a relatively cheap digital camera that can take video.

When you record yourself, you can see where you might be making mistakes. Are you still too slow when drawing a weapon? Do you notice that you are flinching? Are you pulling to the left or right when you fire the gun? Make note of those mistakes and work on correcting them the next time you go shooting. Keep recording your sessions to see your improvement over time.

## *Secret #7: Take It Slow*

Take it slow and get to know the weapons and how to control them. Use the drills here and keep an eye out for more drills that you can try as you work to improve your skills on the range. Rushing through your training will likely result in bad habits that will hamper your skills and will be difficult to break later. Using the techniques and tips we've discussed, including recording yourself, can help you spot these bad habits early.

You can find great tips at AmericanRifleman.org and PoliceMag. com.

# CHAPTER 7:

# Safety

Firearms can be dangerous in the wrong hands. The "wrong hands" does not just mean the hands of a criminal. It also refers to those who are irresponsible with their firearms. Horror stories of irresponsible gun owners are far too common. You do not want to fall into that category, so make sure you follow The Four Rules of Gun Safety.

## *The Four Rules of Safety*

### *Rule #1: Treat the Gun as If It Were Loaded*

You must always treat every gun you touch and that is in your presence, as if it were loaded. It does not matter if you just put the gun down for a few seconds. You should always perform a safety check when you pick it up. Always. There are zero exceptions to this rule.

### *Rule #2: Never Point the Gun at Something You*

## Do Not Intend to Shoot

Even after you have completed the safety check and you are sure there are no rounds in the firearm, you never want to point the gun at anything you do not want to shoot. It does not matter that you just checked it seconds before. You must always assume the gun is loaded, even when you know it is not. Get this into your head now and always follow the rule.

## Rule #3: Be Certain of Your Target, and What Is Behind the Target

When you are ready to fire a loaded gun, always make sure you are certain of your target, as well as what is behind your target. The real world has physics. An object in motion tends to remain in motion. This includes a bullet. Even if it hits a target, it does not stop. It could still travel through the target and continue for a distance. You need to know what is behind the target, just in case the bullet does pass through it.

Hunting accidents often occur because people break this rule. They do not make sure they are shooting at the correct target – they shoot at movement and what they believe is a deer or boar, for example. Be sure of the target.

## Rule #4: Keep the Finger Off the Trigger Until Your Sights Are on the Target

You never want to put your finger on the trigger until your sights are on the target, which you have already confirmed thanks to Rule #3. If your finger is not on the trigger, a modern firearm will not discharge. Taking your finger away from the trigger and the trigger guard eliminates the chances of a negligent discharge.

Never ignore these rules. Always put them at the forefront of your mind and you will not have any accidents. Think about the stories that you hear about accidental shootings. It is obvious that the owners were not paying attention to these rules.

Now, we still need to talk about safety when the guns are not in your hands. There are plenty of things you can do to help increase firearm safety in your home.

## Gun Storage Rules and Safes

Storing the firearms in a gun safe can greatly reduce the risks associated with unauthorized people gaining access to your firearms. While you want to keep your family safe, you want to make sure the firearm is accessible to you.

## Storage Tips

First, you will want to have your guns in safes or lock boxes and keep them locked. The NRA suggests that you use a secure locking device, such as a trigger or cable lock. You never want to rely on the safety built into a gun. Keep in mind that the cable and trigger locks ensure that the gun does not go off. However, it does not guarantee that the gun can't be stolen. For that, you would need a safe, and we will discuss how to choose a proper safe below.

The NRA also suggests that gun owners keep their gun unloaded until it is ready to be used. This is very important when you are storing your gun at home. However, it wouldn't really make much sense for those who have a concealed carry permit and who are out and armed. Keeping the guns in your home unloaded until you need them can reduce the risk of accidents and injuries, though.

In addition, you should store your ammo and your guns separately from one another. Just make sure you have the capability to get what you need quickly and easily for home defense.

## What to Look for in a Gun Safe

It is impossible to recommend a single perfect gun safe because everyone is different. You have different firearms from your friends. You may have more or fewer guns than they have. You may have more space than they have for storage. Your needs for a gun safe will be different from theirs.

First, consider how many guns you have and how many you are likely to buy. Put these on a list, along with the various accessories you have. This will give you a better idea of how large the safe should be or if you should have more than one safe. Bigger is generally better, as you may want to store more than just your firearms in the safe. It also allows you to expand your collection easily.

Always choose a safe that has a thick steel door – at least a quarter of an inch or better. Thick walls are essential as well. Make sure the safe has a quality build and that it will not be easy for a thief to break into even with a pry bar. Get a high fire rating that will keep your guns safe for at least an hour.

In addition to the large standing safes, consider hidden safes. You can find some interesting options from Covert Cabinets, for example. These hidden gun storage areas can work well for many homes. However, you really do need to think about the other members of the family first to see if this would be an appropriate solution.

## *Safety with Kids and Other Family Members*

You should always be extremely careful when it comes to safety and the storage of your firearms. This is true whether you have children or other family members in your home or not. When you are adamant about proper storage and safety, your firearms can pose no danger and they cannot fall into the wrong hands.

Many people out there who are against the Second Amendment say that they are "doing it for the children". They worry kids are getting a hold of guns and hurting themselves and others. It is true that this does happen. It happens because those who own the firearms are not taking proper care of them. They are allowing the accidents to occur. If they were following the Four Rules and storing their guns properly, this would not be a problem.

There are always those kids and family members who might be curious about the guns, of course. This could pose a problem, but if you are locking them up, while keeping the ammunition separate, you should never have any accidents.

## Family Training

One of the best ways to keep the entire family safe is to make sure everyone has a healthy respect for firearms. They should also know how to use firearms. Seek professional training for your family. Perhaps take family members hunting once they have gone through safety and shooting courses. It can provide them with the real-life respect they need around firearms. They will have a much better understanding that the firearm is a tool and that it has the potential to be dangerous when used improperly.

Of course, depending on the age of the child or the mental capacity of the family member, this might not be appropriate and it's up to you to use your best judgment in this matter.

## CHAPTER 8:

# Gun Selection

D o you know which gun you should be using for different situations? What type of gun is right for your needs? This will depend on a range of factors, and in this chapter, we will be looking at the options you have for firearms. We will explore which guns are best for your intended uses and which options are better for an SHTF scenario. You will find that having access to more than one type of firearm is generally best simply because a single firearm is not going to work for everything.

## Key Factors to Consider

Here are the 4 key aspects you need to consider when choosing a firearm:

- Widespread
- Easy to Use
- Ammo Easy to Find
- Fit for Purpose

You want to choose guns that are widespread for several reasons. You will be able to find people who can help you learn how to use the weapon properly. You can also find those who can repair the gun if needed. While it might be fun to have guns that are rare, it could also be a liability. Replacement parts, accessories or repairs will be more difficult to come by with rare firearms.

In addition to having firearms that have seen widespread use in the United States, you will also want to make sure that you have firearms that are easy to use. Think about all aspects of using the gun. How easy is it to load and unload? What is the recoil like? How difficult will the gun be to clean? Do the accessories on the gun make it easier to use or do they complicate the experience?

The guns you choose, especially for defense, or survival for that matter, need to pass the ease of use test.

What about the ammunition? By choosing a widespread and common type of firearm, and caliber, you will find that locating ammunition will be easier. This is true if you happen to be in a SHTF scenario, if you are simply buying ammo to have on hand, or for shooting targets or hunting.

Uncommon types of ammunition tend to be more difficult to locate and this problem is likely to grow more pronounced in areas where laws become stricter, such as California.

The following are some of the most common calibers.

| Handguns: | Rifles: | Shotguns: |
|---|---|---|
| • .22 caliber | • .22 LR | • 16-gauge |
| • 9 mm | • .223 | • 12-gauge |
| • .22 caliber | • .30-60 | |
| • .38 caliber | • .308 | |
| • .40 caliber | • 5.56 mm NATO | |
| • .45 caliber | • 7.62 mm NATO | |

You also want to be sure the firearms you have are *fit for your need*. We will be covering this more in the following section.

## Shotguns, Handguns, and Rifles
In this section, we will be looking at shotguns, handguns and rifles to give you a better perspective on which guns are right for different situations. Later in the book, we've included a list of the top firearms manufacturers for your reference.

## Handguns
Handguns are very popular and they are often the first type of gun someone buys. This is because so many people are buying firearms as a means of defense and handguns are ideal for that. Some might even want to get a concealed carry permit.

The first decision you need to make regarding a handgun is whether you want a revolver or a pistol. Which one of these handguns is a better option? The truth is that both can be very effective and they both have certain advantages.

The semi-automatic pistols tend to have lower recoil, they are reliable and the triggers are generally easy to manipulate. They are faster to reload and they can hold more rounds. However, revolvers have their fans. Traditionally, they are a very reliable and there is a certain aesthetic appeal to them.

For self-defense and home defense, though, most people will tend to gravitate more toward the semi-automatic pistols rather than revolvers. It is a good idea to shoot with each to get a feel for which one you prefer. Ultimately, you want to have a handgun that you like, that feels good in your hand and that you can trust. That is the gun for you, regardless of whether it is a pistol or revolver.

Some of the most popular handguns today include those that fall into the 9mm, .40, and .45 caliber range and that are from Glock, Taurus, Ruger, Beretta, H&K. and Sig Sauer. You can find plenty of quality models that could work well for you.

To learn more about handguns, visit Glock.com and GunsandAmmo.com.

## *Rifles*

Having a rifle is important whether you are a hunter or you are choosing a gun that can help defend your property. Plenty of different options are available.

Those who plan to shoot at further distances may want to consider a bolt action rifle. They tend to weigh a bit more, but they also have better accuracy when you are firing at longer ranges.

Rifles that have shorter barrels, carbines, can still be used at range. However, they can also be used for closer contact situations. In fact, these semi-automatic rifles have even been used successfully for defense within the home.

A 30-30 lever action is a nice gun, too. They tend to be lightweight and easy to carry and are easy to find. They are rugged and dependable. You can find some wonderful options from Winchester.

Is a .22 worth your time? These rifles are often overlooked because of the small caliber, but they can be a fantastic addition to the firearms you own. The ammunition is easy to find and there is plenty of it. In addition, it also happens to be cheap. These rifles are fun and easy to shoot. They do well for hunting

small game including birds, squirrels and rabbits.

Consider one of the popular options, such as an AR-15, Remington 700 bolt action rifle, the Marlin 1895G 45-70 or a Marlin 336 30/30.

Learn more about rifles at Hunter-Ed.com, GirlsJustWannaHaveGuns.com. You can also learn more about ammo for rifles at Ammo.org.

## Shotguns

Shotguns come in many forms and different types work better for different applications.

- **Single Shot** – This type of shotgun features a single barrel that has a break action. You can load and shoot just one shell at a time. To be honest, this is not an ideal firearm for defense or hunting. You may have to engage more targets in a defense situation, and single shot before needing to reload simply won't do.

- **Side by Side** – A side by side shotgun is a type of double-barrel shotgun. This also has a break action, like the single shot, but you can load two shells into the gun at a time. There is a separate trigger for each of the barrels.

- **Over Under** – This is another type of double-barrel shotgun. Again, it has a shell in each barrel and two triggers, allowing for two shots. The barrels, as the name suggests, are placed one over the other. This is often used for competition shooting.

- **Pump** – When it comes to home defense, the pump action, along with the autoloader we will discuss next, are ideal because they tend to have a shorter length. These shotguns have a moveable forearm, which slides back and forth, ejecting the spent shells and replacing them with new shells so you can fire again. In addition to self-defense, many use these for hunting.

- **Autoloader** – This type of shotgun features a tubular

magazine that holds the shells. When you pull the trigger and shoot, the gun ejects the old spent shell and replaces it so you can pull the trigger again. Older autoloader models had spring mechanisms that performed this action, while the new models use a gas system. It works similarly to a semi-auto rifle or handgun.

You can find more information about these types of shotguns at Chuckhawks.com and Gun.Laws.Com.

Many believe shotguns are the ideal solution for both home defense and hunting. They are very easy to clean and maintain thanks to the smooth bore, they shoot slugs or shots and work well for close range engagements, such as defense within your own home. You can use them to hunt for birds, squirrel, and larger game (such as deer) when you are using slugs.

There are many different shotgun models on the market today, but some of the best choices for defense and survival include the Remington 870 pump action shotgun, the Mossberg 500A pump action shotgun and the Remington 1100 semi-automatic shotgun. Those who have the budget might want to consider a Benelli M4, although this is primarily a tactical shotgun.

## Multiple Guns
You might find that having just one type of gun is not enough to satisfy your needs. Choose the gun that you feel is the most important for your first firearm and then add to your collection when you have the money. This is what most people do.

## How To Find Great Deals on Guns
When you are buying firearms, you want to get the best deal possible. This means you might want to consider buying somewhere other than a regular retail shop if you can.
You can check for good deals on firearms at a gun show. You

will find that most states have gun shows, so locating one within driving distance should be easy. In some cases, as we mentioned, you can use the private seller loophole to get the gun that you want. Other times, you will have to facilitate the sale with the help of an FFL when you find a firearm at a show.

# CHAPTER 9:

# Accessories

n this chapter, we will be discussing all the helpful and fun accessories that you can get for handguns, rifles and shotguns. However, please keep in mind that because of certain state laws, some of the items might not be legal for you to purchase and use with your firearm. Check your laws and speak with a gun shop owner to see if you can legally use the accessories that you would like.

## Holsters and Gun Slings

One of the first accessories you will want to have if you are buying a handgun is a holster. This is an essential item if you plan to carry the handgun, whether it is while you are out hunting or for open or concealed carry. As you can imagine, there are countless options when it comes to holsters today.

You can find some classic leather holsters, as well as very modern holster paddles made from molded plastic. There are shoulder holsters, thigh rigs, concealed carry holsters for the waistband, ankle and more.

When you are choosing your holster – or any of your firearm accessories for that matter – make sure you double-check to be certain they work with your gun before buying.

Gun slings are used on your long guns. They allow you to carry the firearm on your person. It will hold the rifle or shotgun in place, so you can free your hands. It provides fast access and it could be a good accessory to consider.

## Extra Magazines

You should also make sure you have some extra magazines for all your firearms that utilize them. This will allow you to have more magazines ready to go for hunting, target practice or for home defense. It also means you will have extra magazines in case the springs in some of your old magazines decide to fail. This doesn't happen often, but when it does, it means the bullets will not be feeding into your gun as quickly as they should and it can cause jams.

## Magazine Cases

You will also want to consider having a magazine case or two. Your magazine will fit right into this case, which simply makes it easier to carry with you so you have easy access. These ensure you have the magazines directly on your person – belt, pack, etc. – and that they are ready to go quickly.

## Lasers and Tactical Lights

You can use lasers on handguns and rifles alike. The lasers, while they are not essential, can be a valuable tool to have. We suggest learning how to shoot and make quick decisions when acquiring targets and firing without a laser first. Then, you can add a laser sight.

Alternatively, some shooters do the opposite. They use the laser sights to help them build muscle memory, which can help them become acclimated to shooting their firearm.

The lasers today are cheaper than they were a decade or so ago and they can make for a nice accessory. Just make sure you do know how to shoot properly without the aid of a laser. You never want to put too much reliance on technology.

## Sights and Scopes

You will find many types of sights and scopes that you could use for the handguns and rifles that you own. Red dot sights and green dot sights, available for rifles and handguns, can help with faster target acquisition. The scopes are great for finding and hitting targets at a long distance, such as when you are out hunting.

These can be very helpful, but we also suggest that you learn how to fire using open sights. Knowing how to use open sights and still hit your target is a skill you will want to develop. You can then add the sights to make things easier. We feel it is a good idea to have the foundation skills in place first, though.

## Grips

You may find that you want to change out the grips on your firearms. The revolver you have might look better with wooden grips, for example. Or, you might decide that you want to have

a tactical grip on your handgun. There are plenty of options out there that can work for your handguns.

You may also want to add something such as an angled grip or a pistol grip to your rifle or shotgun. Make sure the location where you live has not outlawed these types of grips or any of the other accessories you might need for that matter.

## Range Bags

A good range bag is invaluable. You can keep many of your other accessories right in the bag that you take to the range or out to the field for some target practice. They are available in many sizes and styles and you should not have any trouble finding something that will work well for your needs.

## Plenty of Other Options

These are just some of the options available when it comes to firearms accessories. You can find countless other choices out there that might work for your needs. Just make sure you are buying accessories for the right firearm and that they are legal where you live.

## Quality Matters with All Accessories

When you are buying firearms, you want to choose high-quality options. Better quality means better performance and that's what you need from your firearm.

You need to make sure you are putting in just as much due diligence when you are choosing your accessories though. You never want to choose an item for your firearm just because it might be cheaper than some of the other options out there. Quality is always important.

Always take the time to look up some reviews of the product to see what other users are saying about them. You can also speak with some of the other shooters you know and with local gun shop owners. See if they have heard of the product or accessory and what they have to say about it.

It is often worth holding off and buying the better accessory, even if it means waiting to save some more money for it. Make sure the accessory is something that you will use. It can be all too easy to get caught up with buying the latest gear even though you might not really need it.